PORTRAIT OF GOWER
& THE SOUTH WALES COAST

GERAINT TELLEM

HALSGROVE

ACKNOWLEDGEMENTS

I would like to thank my wife Delyth and family for
their continued encouragement and support along with the many
other people who have made this book possible.

Special thanks go to Steven Pugsley, Karen Binaccioni,
Sue Rhodes-Thompson, Denise Lyons and their colleagues at Halsgrove.

First published in Great Britain in 2007

Copyright © 2007 text and photographs Geraint Tellem
Website address: www.gtellemphotography.co.uk

British Library Cataloguing-in-Publication Data
A CIP record for this title is available from the British Library

ISBN 978 1 84114 607 2

HALSGROVE
Halsgrove House, Ryelands Industrial Estate,
Bagley Road, Wellington, Somerset TA21 9PZ
Tel: 01823 653777 Fax: 01823 216796
email: sales@halsgrove.com website: www.halsgrove.com

Printed and bound by D'Auria Industrie Grafiche, Italy

Contents

Introduction   5

The Severn Estuary to Swansea   7

Gower   63

Carmarthen Bay to St David's Head   105

Photographic Notes   144

This book is dedicated to the memory of my grandmother,
Olive Mills 1916 – 2007

Introduction

From the mudflats of the Severn Estuary to the rugged grandeur of the Pembrokeshire shoreline, South Wales boasts some of the most spectacular coastal scenery in the UK. For much of its length, the shape of the coastline has been determined by the Bristol Channel, which has the second-largest tidal range in the world – the largest being the Bay of Fundy in Nova Scotia, Canada. The Channel eventually merges with the open waters of the Atlantic Ocean.

This book is primarily a photographic study of the stunning variety of coastal features that adorn the southern fringes of Wales, with particular emphasis on the rich and diverse geological heritage that dominates this entire stretch of coast. Several urban and industrial areas are also featured as they form an integral part of the coastal landscape, namely Newport, Cardiff, Port Talbot and Swansea.

The first issue to address was deciding where to start and finish the project. I quickly realised that no study of this stretch of coastline would be complete without including the upper reaches of the Severn Estuary, where the tidal influences mentioned above produce the extraordinary phenomenon of the Severn Bore. The journey therefore begins on the English side of the border in Gloucestershire and, continuing westward, ends some 220 miles later at St David's Head, Pembrokeshire, after which the coastline sets a determined course to the north-east.

Approximately midway between these two extremities, and extending some 19 miles to the west of Swansea, lies the Gower peninsula. This was Britain's first designated Area of Outstanding Natural Beauty and is famed for its magnificent beaches and precipitous limestone cliffs. In addition, moorland and marshland, medieval castles, churches, burial tombs and standing stones combine to make this one of the most unique and unexpectedly remote areas of Wales.

Compiling the pictures for this book presented a number of challenges, not least the one faced by any landscape photographer – that of being in the right place at the right time for optimum light conditions. With a book of this nature, this did not necessarily mean waiting for a cloudless sunny day! I have attempted, as far as possible, to portray the area in a wide variety of lighting and weather conditions. Many of the pictures were shot after lengthy periods of waiting on windswept cliff-tops or beaches, and repeated visits to particular locations were often necessary to try and achieve the desired result.

The selection process also presented a dilemma – which areas to include and which to leave out. Some readers may feel that certain important locations have been omitted. However, I soon accepted that it would be impossible to cover everywhere, especially as, despite being a native of South Wales, I currently live a considerable distance away! Inevitably, the logistics of travel, time factors and deadlines have resulted in some specific areas being more intensively represented than others.

I experienced many rewards working on this book, but maybe the most memorable times were those spent hiking through some of the most breathtaking scenery in the country, albeit carrying around 20kg of camera equipment in my rucksack! Having started the project in the belief that I was well acquainted with my subject, I was continually amazed to discover secluded bays, coves and pristine beaches, which I previously never knew existed.

Geraint Tellem

MAP OF GOWER & THE SOUTH WALES COAST

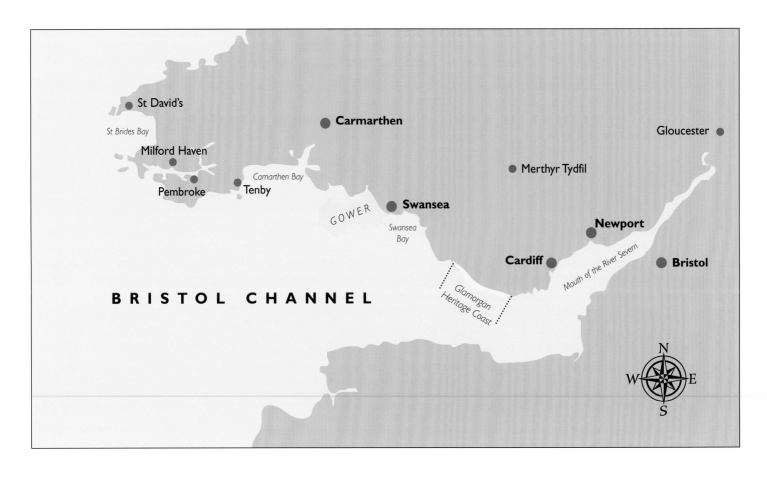

St David's

St Brides Bay

Carmarthen

Milford Haven

Gloucester

Camarthen Bay

Pembroke

Tenby

Merthyr Tydfil

GOWER

Swansea

Swansea Bay

Newport

Cardiff

Mouth of the River Severn

Bristol

BRISTOL CHANNEL

Glamorgan Heritage Coast

N
W E
S

THE SEVERN ESTUARY TO SWANSEA

The village of Minsterworth in Gloucestershire may seem an unlikely place to start a journey along the coast of South Wales. This, however, is one of the best places to observe the spectacular Severn Bore. The surge wave is a direct result of the massive tidal range in the Bristol Channel, combined with the sudden decrease in depth and dramatic narrowing of the Severn Estuary. At spring tides around the equinoxes in March and September, waves as high as 9ft have been recorded.

Between the Severn Bridges and Cardiff, the coast sinks below sea level in many places, protected from flooding by a long sea wall. The estuary itself is one of the most important marine conservation sites in Britain. Extensive intertidal mudflats, rocky platforms, sandbanks and salt marshes are home to internationally important populations of waterfowl, invertebrates and migratory fish.

Perhaps the most dramatic change to this part of the coastline in recent years has been the regeneration of Cardiff Bay, Europe's largest waterfront development and home to the Welsh Assembly. The construction of a barrage has created a vast freshwater lake and the area around the bay is now one of Cardiff's most exciting attractions with its modern apartment blocks, entertainment complexes and cosmopolitan café culture.

West of Cardiff, the coastline assumes an entirely different character as the geology changes. Limestone cliffs, picturesque bays and wide sandy beaches now define the landscape – the 14 mile Glamorgan Heritage Coast between Aberthaw and Ogmore-by Sea is particularly scenic. The remains of what was once Britain's largest sand dune system can be found near Porthcawl, at Merthyr Mawr Warren and Kenfig. This system once stretched continuously to Mumbles. Further westwards, the stark outline of Port Talbot Steelworks interrupts the skyline, before the coast curves around Swansea Bay towards Gower.

Severn Bore at Minsterworth.
'When the bore comes, the stream does not swell by degrees, as at other times,
but rolls in with a head … foaming and roaring as though it were enraged by
the opposition which it encounter' – Thomas Harrel, 1824.

The Severn Bore.
The Severn Bore is one of the biggest of around 60 such phenomena that occur worldwide.
Other famous examples are on the Seine and Gironde in France, the Amazon in Brazil, the
Indus in India and the Petitcodiac, New Brunswick. By far the largest is the Ch'ient'ang'kian
(Hang-chou-fe) in China. At spring tide the wave attains a height of up to 25ft (7.5m) and a
speed of 13-15 knots (24-27km/h). It is heard advancing at a range of 14 miles (22.5km).

River Severn at Minsterworth.
After the arrival of the bore the river floods rapidly,
high tide being reached approximately sixty minutes later.

Surfers at Newnham.
The river narrows dramatically at this point and it is a popular place for surfers attempting endurance
records. There is a splendid view of the bore here as it sweeps rapidly over the broad sands.

The *Severn Princess*.
This is the largest of three ferries (the others being the *Severn King* and *Queen*) that operated between Beachley and Aust between 1934 and 1966. Launched in 1959, she carried up to 17 vehicles. She was rescued from a scrap yard in Ireland and towed back to Wales in 1999. The vessel is now being restored in Chepstow.

Severn Bridge from Beachley.
Opened by the Queen on 8 September 1966, the bridge is 5240ft (1597m) long and the span between the two towers stretches 3240ft (988m). It was the seventh longest bridge in the world at the time of construction.

Severn Bridge.
The steel towers are 445ft (136m) above mean high water and are of hollow box construction.

The Severn Estuary at Beachley.
The maximum tidal range of the estuary occurs close to the village of Beachley.
This photograph was taken on the morning of an equinoctial spring tide (the Severn
Bore pictured on page 9 occurred an hour or so later) – the speed of the incoming
current is awe-inspiring. For comparison, the photograph on the next page
illustrates the extent to which the estuary drains at extreme low tide.

**Low tide,
Severn Estuary.**

Second Severn Crossing.
This was opened in June 1996 to augment the traffic capacity of the existing Severn Bridge. It is 3.1 miles (5.1km)
long and consists of a 456m central span over the 'Shoots' channel and approach viaducts on either side.

**Tidal mudflats
near the Second
Severn Crossing.**

Sunrise over the Severn Estuary from Goldcliff, near Newport.

Remains of salmon traps at Goldcliff near Newport. Goldcliff has long been associated with the tidal fishing of salmon. The technique uses the so-called 'putcher' baskets traditionally made from hazel rods and withy (willow) plait, which are set out against the ebb tide in huge wooden 'ranks'.

Goldcliff near Newport.

Newport Transporter Bridge.
Opened in 1906. The design of the bridge was chosen because the riverbanks are very low at
the desired crossing point. The only other such bridge in the UK is in Middlesborough.

Cardiff Bay.
Since 1987, this area has been redeveloped beyond all
recognition. It is now one of the main cultural centres of Cardiff.

Dawn over Penarth Pier.
Often referred to as Cardiff's 'Garden by the Sea' because of its beautiful gardens and
wide-open spaces, Penarth is also famed for its Victorian/Edwardian architecture.
The pier was opened in 1895 and the pavilion was added in the 1920s.

Dawn over Penarth Pier.

Lavernock Point.
It was from here in May 1897 that Marconi transmitted the first message by wireless telegraphy across the water to Flatholm 3.5 miles (5.5km) away. The message 'Are you ready?' was to revolutionise communications around the world. A line drawn between Lavernock Point and Sand Point in Somerset marks the lower limit of the Severn Estuary and upper limit of the Bristol Channel.

Sully Island.
This tidal island looks fairly flat and innocuous from the mainland. However, a walk to the opposite (south) side reveals a magnificent rock platform affording extensive views up the Severn Estuary and across the Channel to Devon and Somerset. The bright red rocks are evidence of the arid desert that prevailed during the Permian and Triassic geological periods.

Near St Donats.
The Glamorgan Heritage Coast stretches 14 miles from West Aberthaw to Porthcawl, and features beautiful cliffs towering 200ft high flanked by some of the finest wave-cut limestone platforms in Europe. The alternate layers of limestone and shale give the cliffs their unusually irregular pattern.

Near St Donats, Glamorgan Heritage Coast.

Near St Donats, Glamorgan Heritage Coast.
Freshwater springs seeping from the cliffs have produced
moss and algae growth in a number of places.

Nash Point.
The lighthouse was built in 1832 to mark the treacherous sandbanks offshore.

Nash Point and the Devon/Somerset coastline.

Dusk over the Bristol Channel from near Nash Point.

The hills of Exmoor from Nash Point.

Traeth Mawr at dusk, near Nash Point.

Cliff erosion at
Traeth Bach.

**Limestone pillar,
Traeth Bach.**

Cliffs near
Traeth Mawr.

**Low tide,
Traeth Mawr.**

**Traeth Bach near
Southerndown.**

Looking south-east from near Trwyn y Witch, Southerndown.
A fine cliff-top path leads to Nash Point, seen here in the distance.

Dunraven Bay, Southerndown.
An expansive beach is exposed here at low tide. This is one of the best areas to find fossils, although care should be taken, as the crumbling layers are prone to landslides.

Limestone cliffs at Dunraven Bay, Southerndown.

Dunraven Bay, Southerndown.

Sunset from Dunraven Bay, Southerndown.

View across the Bristol Channel from Ogmore-by-Sea.

Winter afternoon
sunlight on
the cliffs near
Ogmore-by-Sea.

**The Ogmore
Estuary in winter.**

The flood plain of the River Ogmore.

Sand dunes at Merthyr Mawr Warren.
The biggest sand dune in Europe is located near here – known locally as 'The Big Dipper'.

**Winter sunrise over
Porthcawl Pier.**

Stormy seas at Porthcawl.

Rock Samphire
(*Crithmum Maritimum*) at
Rest Bay, Porthcawl.

Low tide at Rest Bay, Porthcawl.

Dusk at Rest Bay, Porthcawl.

**Kenfig Dunes
near Port Talbot.**
Kenfig National Nature
Reserve is one of the most
significant sites in the UK
for nature conservation. It
is home to unique wild
orchids as well as insects
and wildlife.

Sunset over Kenfig Pool.
This is the largest natural freshwater lake in South Wales and it is a
particularly important stopping-off area for migrating birds.

Kenfig Pool at twilight.

Port Talbot Steelworks.
The original steelworks were built in 1901 when the area was renowned
worldwide for its coal and steel. The integrated Abbey Works
of the Steel Company of Wales were built in 1947.

Swansea Bay from Aberavon beach.

Swansea Marina.
Opened in the 1980s, this area has been described as 'the jewel in the city centre's crown'.
The opening of the National Waterfront Museum in October 2005, together with a number
of cafés and fashionable shops, has given the marina a very cosmopolitan atmosphere.

Evening light, Swansea Marina.

GOWER

Standing at the summit of Rhossili Down, looking out over one of the most stunning beaches in the country, it is easy to understand why Gower has long been designated an Area of Outstanding Natural Beauty. Indeed, it is hard to travel very far throughout the peninsula without stumbling on similar scenes of breathtaking beauty.

Gower can effectively be divided into three main sections. Firstly, the precipitous south coast characterised by limestone crags, especially at the western end towards Worms Head. Secondly, the central plateau of Cefn Bryn rising to around 500ft – this is an area of rugged moorland, ancient stone cairns and panoramic views, which on clear days, extend to Pembrokeshire and Devon as well as the whole of Gower. Finally, the quieter north coast, fringed with marshes and mudflats where wild horses, sheep and cattle graze among the many inlets and sand dunes that meander into the landscape from the Lougher Estuary.

The name 'Gower' is thought to be a derivative of the term 'Meini Gwyr', meaning 'Land of the stone men'. Indeed, many parts of North Gower are notable for standing stones, the most well known being Arthur's Stone on Cefn Bryn. However, it is now widely accepted that Gwyr is of early descriptive origin, and probably refers to the shape of the Gower peninsula itself. Incidentally, the area is often mistakenly referred to as 'The Gower' whereas the correct name is simply 'Gower'.

West of Mumbles, the limestone cliffs are punctuated at regular intervals by the wide sandy bays for which Gower is famed, such as Langland, Caswell, Oxwich, Three Cliffs, Mewslade and finally, as the coastline veers north, Rhossili, which faces the open Atlantic. After rounding the promontory of Burry Holms, the sand dunes of Whiteford Burrows and the vast Llanrhidian Marsh contrast completely with the drama of the cliffs to the south. The whole of North Gower is a haven for birdwatchers and naturalists alike.

Mumbles Pier at dusk.
The 225m long (835ft) pier was built in 1898.
There has been a lifeboat station here since 1835.

Mumbles Head.
The first lighthouse was constructed in 1794 to guide vessels along
the coast and into Swansea Bay past the Mixon shoal, half a mile to the south.

Mumbles Head.

Caswell Bay.

Three Cliffs Bay.
One of the most popular and picturesque beaches in Gower the bay is accessed by numerous footpaths,
notably along the valley of Pennard Pill that leads to the bay from the nearest main road.

Three Cliffs Bay.
The bay is surrounded by sand dunes and at low tide it is possible to walk under the cliffs through an archway.

Three Cliffs Bay.

Three Cliffs Bay.

Port Eynon Point.
The most southerly point in Gower and a very popular tourist area.
From here, the coast runs north-west towards Worms Head and
offers some of the best cliff-top scenery in Gower.

Cliffs near Paviland Cave, Gower. There are around 95 caves of note in Gower and Paviland (also known as 'Goat's Hole') has become the most famous following the discovery of a 29,000-year-old human skeleton there in 1823. At the time of the burial, the cave would have been around 70 miles inland, overlooking a plain.

Mewslade Bay.
Surrounded by towering limestone cliffs, this secluded bay is one of the prettiest in Gower.

Mewslade Bay.
Winter storms often lead
to significant sand shift on
the beach, exposing
outcrops of jagged
limestone underneath.

Mewslade Bay.

Mewslade Bay.

Low tide at Mewslade and Fall Bays.

Wave patterns at
Mewslade Bay.

The south-west coast of Gower from Tears Point near Fall Bay.

Breaking wave, South Gower.

Sunset over Worms Head.
Rhossili Bay and Worms Head, at the western tip of Gower, must surely rank amongst
the best coastal locations in the UK. The breathtaking views of towering cliffs and the vast
beach make this a popular place for hikers, surfers and paragliders.

Worms Head from Rhossili Down.
This headland is separated from the mainland by a causeway,
which is only accessible for two and a half hours, either side of low tide.

**Looking towards
Worms Head.**

Midsummer sunset over Worms Head.
A hike to the Outer Head, although difficult in places, is an unforgettable experience.

The village of Rhossili
and Worms Head from
Rhossili Down.

The wreck of *Helvetia* and Worms Head.
The *Helvetia* sank in a gale in November 1887.

Rhossili Beach.
The three-mile long beach curves northwards to another tidal island at Burry Holms.
Behind the beach is Rhossili Down which at 193m (633ft), is the highest point in Gower.

Looking towards Burry Holms from Rhossili Down.

**Rock pools,
Burry Holms.**

Sand dunes at Broughton Bay.

Whiteford Burrows.

Whiteford Sands and Burrows.
This dune and pine plantation is one of the many nature reserves on the Gower peninsula.

View over
Whiteford Sands
and the Lougher
Estuary.

**Thrift *(Armeria Maritima)* forms a carpet of pink across
Llanrhidian Marsh in early summer.**

Llanrhidian Marsh.
The marsh, which occupies much of the North Gower coast is renowned for its abundant bird-life including herons, buzzards and wildfowl.

Llanrhidian Marsh.
The marsh is frequently
flooded at high tide.

**Decaying boat,
Llanrhidian Marsh.**

Ragged Robin *(Lynchnis Flos Cuculi)* **in a forest of rushes, Llanrhidian Marsh.**

Weobley Castle.
Dating from the fourteenth century, the castle stands on an escarpment
overlooking the bleak expanses of Llanrhidian Marsh. It served
more as a fortified manor house than a serious military establishment.

**Jet skier,
Lougher Estuary.**

Lougher Estuary at sunset from Penclawdd.

Arthur's Stone.
The Gower peninsula is littered with dolmens, standing stones
and other prehistoric remains. Arthur's Stone on Cefn Bryn is probably the
most well known throughout Wales. The burial chamber dates from at least
4000BC and weighs over 25 tons.

Broad Pool.
Habitat for amphibians, dragon flies and wetland birds, Broad Pool lies in a shallow
basin on the limestone plateau below Cefn Bryn. Its origin appears to be natural.

CAMARTHEN BAY TO ST DAVID'S HEAD

West of Gower, Carmarthen Bay sweeps around in a gentle curve towards Tenby, which, on a clear day, is visible in the far distance. The eastern end of the bay is dominated by the vast stretches of sand at Cefn Sidan and Pendine, which are separated by the estuaries of the Tywi, Taf and Gwendraeth. In contrast, rocky wooded hillsides form the main backdrop to the coastline as it veers south towards Saundersfoot.

The 186-mile Pembrokeshire coastal path starts at Amroth, much of it at cliff top level. It passes through seventeen sites of scientific interest and several nature reserves, as well as providing superb coastal views.

Tenby may be regarded as the gateway to the Pembrokeshire Coast National Park, Britain's only truly coastal National Park, designated in 1952. Without a doubt, the most notable features of the Pembrokeshire coastline are the cliffs, which have been subject to continual erosion from the pounding sea. Between these cliffs are numerous sheltered coves, pristine sandy beaches, mudflats, dunes and deep wooded estuaries, the best example of the latter being the vast Milford Haven waterway. Although a mere mile and a half wide at its entrance, it extends inland for some 20 miles and its deep water channel led to the area's emergence as Britain's leading oil port and the second largest in Europe by the 1970s. The port is also now a major centre for the regasification and distribution of Liquid Natural Gas (LNG).

The coastline in the extreme south west resembles that of Cornwall, especially around the Marloes Peninsula and St David's Head. Tumultuous jagged headlands thrust out into the Atlantic Ocean, fully exposed to the ferocious storms that occur frequently, especially in winter.

Offshore, several islands are internationally renowned for their seabird and seal populations, the largest of which are Skomer, Skokholm, Ramsey, Grasholm and Caldey.

Sand dunes at Pembrey.
The eight-mile long Pembrey beach (or Cefn Sidan Sands) and Pendine Sands further west, are amongst the largest beaches in the UK. There are extensive views across Carmarthen Bay to Tenby and Gower. Both beaches are famous for land-speed record attempts, the most notable by Malcolm Cambell, who reached 174.22 mph (280.38kmh) in February 1927.

Sand dunes at Pembrey.

Laugharne.
Immortalised by the poet
Dylan Thomas (1914–53)
who lived here in a boat-
house for the last four
years of his life,
Laugharne is now a
paradise for writers,
walkers, sailors,
fishermen and artists.

Tenby Harbour.
One of the principal tourist resorts in West Wales, Tenby nestles between
two fine beaches on a natural promontory overlooking Carmarthen Bay. A few miles offshore
lies the monastic Caldey Island, popular with visitors on day-trips from Tenby harbour.

Sand dunes at
Broadhaven.

Cliffs near Barafundle Bay.

Barafundle Bay.
This is one of the finest beaches in Pembrokeshire, with
clear water and fine soft sand fringed by wooded cliffs.

Stackpole Head.

Summer wildflowers near St Govan's Head.

**Looking towards
St Govan's Head.**
This headland delineates
the boundary between the
Bristol Channel and the
open Atlantic Ocean.

St Govan's Chapel.
This tiny building was built in the thirteenth century on the
site of the cell of a sixth-century Celtic monk. It is accessed by a steep staircase from
the car park above and legend has it that the number of steps counted on the
way down never matches the number reached on the way up!

Elegug Stacks.
These two detached pillars of limestone are crammed with Guillemots and Razorbills.
Fulmar and Kittewake nest on the cliffs along with Black-Backed and Herring Gulls.

The Green Bridge of Wales.
Situated a little further along the coast from Elegug Stacks, this is
one of the finest natural limestone arches in the country.

Freshwater West.
The beach here is one of
the principal surfing
beaches in Pembrokeshire.

St Ann's Head.
This is statistically the
sunniest place in Wales.

Old Red Sandstone cliff.
St Ann's Head.

Westdale Bay.

Winter sunset at Westdale Bay.

Marloes Sands.
This is a very popular family beach in summer.
It is noted for its cliffs with strange rock formations.

Marloes Sands.

Marloes Sands.

Approaching winter storm near Marloes Sands.

Dusk over Skokholm Island, Pembrokeshire.
The islands of Skokholm, Skomer and tiny Grassholm are home
to some of Europe's most significant sea-bird colonies.

Wooltack Point.

Wooltack Point.

Looking south east along the Pembrokeshire coastline from Wooltack Point.

**Clifftop Thrift
near Solva.**

Ebb tide,
late evening,
Newgale Sands.

Newgale Sands.

Walkers on Newgale Sands.

Ramsey Sound from Pen Dal-aderyn.
This is the most westerly point in Wales. The tidal race through the sound can reach up to
8 knots, especially near the group of rocks known as 'The Bitches'. On a stormy day, the
power of the tide is incredible, creating tumultuous waves, eddies, and whirlpools.

Ramsey Island.
The dual-humped island lies about 1km offshore across Ramsey Sound. Owned by the RSPB, the island has spectacular cliffs teeming with sea birds, as well as one of the largest grey seal colonies in southern Britain.

Ramsey Sound from St Justinian's.

**Looking towards
St David's Head.**

Whitesands Bay and Carn Llidi in early summer.

Whitesands Bay and Ramsey Island from Carn Llidi.
The views from the top of Carn Llidi are extensive and include the whole of St Bride's Bay, the Dewisland Peninsula, St Davids, and parts of the coast leading northwards up to Strumble Head.

**Heather on the slopes
of Carn Llidi near
St David's Head.**

**Looking towards
St David's Head from
Carn Llidi.**

Photographic Notes

The majority of the pictures in this book were taken between March 2005 and June 2007 using a Mamiya RZ Pro II medium-format camera, with 50mm, 90mm and occasionally 180mm lenses. My choice of film was Fujichrome Velvia. At ISO 50 it is relatively slow and is known for unrivalled clarity, sharpness, and vibrant colours.

However, no photographer can ignore the fact that the age of digital capture is now firmly established. Many photographers had already 'gone digital' back in 2005 or earlier, but for much of my landscape work to date I have been reluctant to change completely, preferring to stick with what I know! As a compromise, I decided that the best option whilst working on this book would be to use digital equipment as well, initially using a Canon 10D, and more recently a Canon 5D, with a range of premium lenses. In hindsight this proved to be very beneficial. I found myself in several situations where it simply wasn't practical to shoot medium-format, and on these occasions the speed and flexibility of the digital camera became invaluable. The pictures of the Severn Bore are a case in point.

The incresing demand for digital images from most areas of the photogrpahic industry, together with the incredible quality produced by today's top-of-the-range digital cameras, has finally convinced me to switch almost exclusively to digital photography from now on.

I often use a polarising filter in sunny conditions to eliminate reflections from water, enhance blue sky and remove glare from foliage. An 81B warm-up filter is invaluable for reducing the slightly 'cool' cast the polariser sometimes causes and I occasionally used neutral-density graduated filters when the brightness of the sky needed to be balanced with the landscape, reducing the risk of 'burn out'.

Finally, a sturdy tripod was necessary most of the time – aperture values were generally small for maximum depth of field, resulting in slow shutter speeds especially in low-light conditions.